THE CYBERBULLY DEFENSE HANDBOOK

Protecting Yourself and Your Reputation Online"

MICHAEL C DYSON

CONTENTS

Introduction 1

Run, hide, fight! 2

My experience 3

What is Cyberbullying? 5

How Cyberbullies Operate 8

How cyberbullying differs from traditional bullying 10

The pros and cons of standard cyberbullying advice. 12

Harmful effects of cyberbullying 15

Goals for victims of cyberbullying 17

Getting to know the enemy 19

Identifying and Avoiding Cyberbullies 21

Tracing a fake profile 24

Picking a fake profile 25

Reasons people use a fake profile 27

Identifying and Avoiding Cyberbullies 29

Strategy 32

Essential tools 34

Anger and aggression 39

Aggressive personality types 44

Turn the other cheek 47

Have courage 50

Difference between techniques and tactics 52

Self Defense 56

Responding to an abusive post 58

Responding assertively 61

Boundaries to set and abide by 63

Sample Questions 65

Conclusion 67

Examples of cyberbullying 69

Examples including responses 74

INTRODUCTION

Welcome to the Cyberbully Self-Defense Handbook. In this guide, we will explore the world of cyberbullying and provide strategies for defending yourself against this type of aggression. Cyberbullying can be a daunting and hurtful experience, but with the right tools and mindset, you can confront it head-on and protect yourself from its harmful effects.

One of the critical principles of cyberbullying selfdefense is understanding the nature of this type of aggression. Cyberbullying is not just name-calling or insults but rather a deliberate attempt to hurt or humiliate someone online. This often takes the form of repeated attacks on a person's character or reputation, leaving victims feeling isolated, powerless, and vulnerable.

In this guide, we will teach you how to strategically use specific questions that will shine a light on the bully's behavior and deflect the insult or threat away from you. By understanding cyberbullies' tactics, you can respond assertively, confidently, and effectively.

Remember, cyberbullying is not something that you have to face alone. By using the strategies outlined in this guide and seeking support from trusted friends, family, or professionals, you can defend yourself against cyberbullying and emerge stronger and more resilient than ever before.

RUN, HIDE, FIGHT!

Run, hide, fight is a set of guidelines developed to help people respond to an active shooter situation. It emphasizes three basic options: run to escape the threat, hide from the shooter, or fight back against the attacker as a last resort.

These principles are based on the fight or flight response, a natural physiological reaction to a perceived threat. In some situations, the body may also respond with a third option, freeze, which is when a person becomes immobilized and unable to move or respond.

The run, hide, and fight principles are designed to help people overcome the freeze response and take action to protect themselves in a dangerous situation. While these guidelines were developed for active shooter situations, they can also be applied to other situations where a person may feel threatened or in danger.

I am writing this book with this principle firmly in mind. I want to help people not feel helpless, hopeless, or powerless in protecting themselves from cyberbullying.

MY EXPERIENCE

Sitting alone in my study, I received a notification on my phone. It was a link to another post naming me on social media, and my anger grew as I read the lies being spread about me. The post was another of many that accused me of being a mass murderer responsible for killing 35 people in the Port Arthur massacre, which was completely untrue.

I felt like I had been punched in the head from behind and falling into a deep, dark pit of anger and aggression because these posts were becoming more frequent and persistent. For a moment, I was utterly consumed by the emotional intensity of the situation. I felt defenseless because the author of the writing was anonymous and beyond my physical reach.

After seeking expert advice and receiving no helpful response, I realized I couldn't let the lies and allegations destroy my reputation. Rather than appearing upset or angry, I decided to take a more strategic approach to counteract the damage done. I aimed to shift the focus away from me and onto the authors of the false claims. By responding assertively and confidently, I could show that the lies and allegations were baseless and reflected more on the authors than me. Ultimately, I aimed to stop the conspiracy theory or, at the very least, remove myself from it.

By exploring the depths of language and writing techniques, I was able to find a way to fight back against the written aggression and abuse that had been directed toward me.

Being a police officer, I had extensive experience in dealing with physical aggression, but I realized that I needed to find a way to apply that knowledge to written attacks. So, I started to educate myself on the literature surrounding verbal self-defense techniques and assertive writing. As I learned more about these techniques, I responded more effectively to insults and accusations. Rather than responding in anger out of frustration, I responded calmly and assertively, using the language and writing techniques I had learned.

Through daily practice on social media, I sharpened my skills and gradually became more effective in defeating challenging posts and comments that I would otherwise find very offensive and harmful.

While I can't guarantee that this process will be effortless for everyone, it does require patience and time to choose the right words and context to reflect bullying comments on the authors. It's important to realize that the internet not only provides a secure space for these bullies but also for you to leverage. By taking control of the situation and responding assertively, you can come out of any exchange with honor and integrity while the bully is exposed for their true nature. So, don't let written aggression or abuse destroy your reputation or self-esteem. Educate yourself, practice assertive writing, and take control of the situation. By writing this book, I hope that I have been helpful.

WHAT IS CYBERBULLYING?

Cyberbullying is a form of online harassment that can take many forms and have serious adverse effects on victims. In this chapter, we will explore what cyberbullying is, the different forms it can take, and its effects on victims.

Cyberbullying means using digital technology, such as social media, text messaging, and email, to harass, intimidate, or harm someone. Unlike traditional bullying, which may occur face-to-face and in person, cyberbullying can occur 24/7 and from anywhere. Cyberbullies may use a variety of tactics to target their victims, including spreading rumors, sharing private information, making threats, or creating fake social media accounts.

There are several different forms of cyberbullying, including these common types that I have experienced:

- **<u>Harassment</u>** includes repeatedly sending threatening or abusive messages or posting negative comments on someone's social media accounts.
- **<u>Cyberstalking</u>** is using technology to monitor someone's online activity, track their movements, or gather personal information about them.

- **Impersonation** involves creating fake social media accounts or email addresses to impersonate someone and post false or damaging information about them.
- **Doxxing** is publishing someone's private information online, such as their home address or phone number, without their consent.
- **Exclusion** involves intentionally excluding someone from online groups or conversations or blocking them from social media accounts.

Cyberbullying can have serious adverse effects on victims, including:

- **Emotional Distress**: Victims of cyberbullying may experience anxiety, depression, low self-esteem, and other emotional problems due to the harassment.
- **Social Isolation:** Cyberbullying can lead to social isolation, as victims may feel too embarrassed or ashamed to interact with others.
- **Physical Health Problems:** The stress of cyberbullying can also lead to physical health problems, such as headaches, stomachaches, and difficulty sleeping.
- **Academic or Work Performance:** Cyberbullying can also affect victims' academic or work performance, as they may be too distracted or upset to focus on their responsibilities.

Cyberbullying can have severe and long-lasting impacts on victims, and seeking help is crucial in dealing with the problem. However, it can be challenging for victims to receive the support they need as the severity of the situation is often downplayed or overlooked by others. The standard advice of "ignore it, block it, or report it" may not be effective for everyone and can leave victims feeling helpless. Therefore, it is essential to provide tailored support and guidance to victims of cyberbullying, acknowledging the seriousness of their situation and providing practical steps to address the issue.

By understanding what cyberbullying is, the different forms it can take, and its effects on victims, we can begin to take steps to protect ourselves against it and provide support to others who have been targeted. The next chapter will explore how cyberbullies operate and their tactics to harass their victims.

HOW CYBERBULLIES OPERATE

Cyberbullies use a range of tactics and methods to harass and intimidate their targets. This chapter will explore some of the most common tactics and methods cyberbullies use and how cyberbullying differs from traditional bullying.

- **Anonymous Communication:** Cyberbullies often use anonymous communication to hide their identity and avoid getting caught. They may use fake profiles, email addresses, or phone numbers to harass their targets.

- **Public Humiliation:** Cyberbullies may use social media platforms to shame or embarrass their targets publicly. They may share embarrassing photos or videos or post hurtful comments or messages on public forums.

- **Cyberstalking:** Cyberbullies may engage in cyberstalking, monitoring their targets' online activity or tracking their movements. They may use this information to intimidate or harass their targets further.

- **Threats:** Cyberbullies may use threats to intimidate their targets. They may threaten physical harm, spread rumors or lies, or threaten to release private information.

- **Exclusion**: Cyberbullies may use exclusion as a tactic, intentionally leaving their targets out of online groups or conversations or blocking them from social media accounts.

Blocking, ignoring, or reporting cyberbullying attacks may seem like a straightforward solution to the problem, but unfortunately, it may not always work. Cyberbullies are often very persistent and may continue to harass and abuse their victims even if they are blocked or ignored. They may even escalate their attacks by targeting their victim's friends, groups, employers, or others in their social circle. This can be especially damaging, as it can cause the victim to feel isolated and alone and may even result in job loss or other negative consequences. It is important to remember that seeking help and support might not always be the best way to deal with your personal situation.

HOW CYBERBULLYING DIFFERS FROM TRADITIONAL BULLYING

One of the most significant differences between cyberbullying and face-to-face bullying is the lack of personal confrontation and the threat of physical harm.

The anonymous nature of cyberbullying creates a sense of uncertainty and fear for victims, as they are left in the dark about the identity and motives of their aggressor. The lack of knowledge about their enemy and their capabilities can be particularly distressing, as it leaves victims in a constant state of alertness and anxiety.

Moreover, cyberbullying can be insidious and more harmful than traditional forms of bullying. Negative messages or images can have a long-lasting impact and be difficult to erase from the internet. The fear caused by not knowing your enemy can make cyberbullying a particularly traumatic experience. Having a measure of control over the situation is crucial for victims to overcome the psychological effects of this type of abuse.

While the options for victims of cyberbullying may be limited, it's important to remember that sometimes fighting back can be the best course of action. Unlike face-to-face bullying, victims of cyberbullying may not have the same opportunities to avoid or run away from confrontation.

However, the first steps victims can take to protect themselves are those commonly recommended; blocking, ignoring, seeking legal action, or enlisting the support of others to help put a stop to the abuse.

THE PROS AND CONS OF STANDARD CYBERBULLYING ADVICE.

I tried all the advice to counter cyberbullying. That included reporting attacks to the State and Federal police. I complained to Facebook but got no response, so I went to the national media to highlight the lack of attention given to false and defamatory posts and pages on Facebook. My story made national and international news, but none of this stopped the attacks or resulted in the removal of any material from Facebook.

These are examples of the problems that I encountered with following the recommended ways to deal with cyberbullying:

Ignore it: The first advice frequently given is to ignore cyberbullying and not engage with the perpetrator. This can prevent the situation from escalating and may cause the bully to lose interest.

Ignoring cyberbullying is not always effective, especially if the perpetrator is persistent. In my experience, when I first received hate mail, emails, and SMS messages, I chose to ignore them. However, as time passed, the attacks escalated. Perpetrators started creating Facebook pages about me, falsely accusing me of being a murderer. The abuse even spread to anonymous threats and abusive messages being sent to people with the same surname as me, regardless of whether they were related to me or not. The situation became so severe that one of my family members had to have their telephone delisted due to the constant nuisance calls they received. Unfortunately, ignoring the initial attacks only emboldened the cyberbullies to intensify their efforts, causing more harm and disruption to my life.

Block or report the bully: Most social media platforms and websites have tools that allow users to block or report individuals who are engaging in cyberbullying. This can help to prevent the bully from contacting you further or spreading harmful messages.

Blocking people who sent me SMS messages and abusive emails had no effect. Those people created new fake identities. Having a business website enabled people to contact me with new identities and email accounts.

Seek support: Talking to a trusted friend, family member, or mental health professional can provide emotional support and guidance on how to deal with cyberbullying.

I reported the abuse and defamatory materials to every authority and to Facebook and received absolutely zero help. Authorities advised me to ignore it, and Facebook never acknowledged my complaint.

Take legal action: In extreme cases, it may be necessary to take legal action against the cyberbully, particularly if they engage in criminal behavior such as harassment or threats.

Over time two law firms offered to represent me with legal action. However, tracing the culprits privately took a lot of work. Another primary consideration was that the likelihood that the culprits had anything worth suing them for was virtually zero.

Respond assertively: Sometimes, responding assertively to the cyberbully can be an effective strategy. This involves calmly and firmly standing up for yourself and setting boundaries around what behavior you will and will not tolerate.

Confronting every one of the cyberbullies, Facebook pages, and internet sites has resulted in me no longer being subject to allegations, abuse, or threats. Internet trolls who attack me appear to resent that I fight back the way I do, but the result is always the same – they disengage as their abuse falls on deaf ears.

When it comes to dealing with cyberbullying, there is no one-size-fits-all approach. The best course of action will depend on the specific circumstances of the situation and what feels most comfortable and empowering for the individual involved. In my own experience, I decided to fight back. I needed to take a stand and turn the tables on my attackers. This decision empowered me and allowed me to take control of the situation. It's essential for victims of cyberbullying to remember that they have options and can choose a path that feels right for them, whether that means seeking support from others or confronting the bully head-on. The most important thing is to take action and not suffer in silence.

HARMFUL EFFECTS OF CYBERBULLYING

Cyberbullying can cause a range of fears and anxieties for people who experience it. Here are some of the main concerns people may have about cyberbullies:

- **Fear of embarrassment:** Cyberbullies may use the internet to publicly shame or embarrass their victims, often through social media or other online platforms. The fear of being humiliated in front of friends, family, or the general public can be a significant concern for cyberbullied people.

- **Fear of isolation:** Cyberbullying can also make people feel isolated and alone. Bullies may use the internet to spread rumors or make negative comments about their victims, leading others to distance themselves from the bullied person.

- **Fear of physical harm:** Cyberbullying can sometimes escalate to physical threats or violence. Victims may fear for their safety and the safety of their loved ones.

- **Fear of online harassment:** Cyberbullies may use multiple online platforms to harass their victims, leaving them feeling like there is no escape from the abuse. The constant barrage of negative messages can be overwhelming and cause significant anxiety.
- **Fear of psychological harm:** Cyberbullying can severely impact a person's mental health and well-being. Victims may experience depression, anxiety, or other psychological issues due to the abuse.

Overall, cyberbullying can create a range of fears and anxieties for those who experience it, and it's essential to address the issue and get help if needed.

GOALS FOR VICTIMS OF CYBERBULLYING

Victims of cyberbullying may hope to achieve various outcomes depending on their specific situation and the severity of the bullying. Here are some common goals that victims of cyberbullying may hope to achieve:

- **To stop bullying:** The primary goal for cyberbullying victims is often to end the harassment. They may seek help from authorities, such as school officials, law enforcement, or online platforms, to stop the bully from continuing to target them.

- **To seek justice:** Victims may want the bully to face the consequences for their actions, such as legal action, suspension, expulsion from school or work, or the removal of the bully's online accounts or posts.

- **To feel safe:** Victims of cyberbullying may feel unsafe and anxious due to the bullying. They may hope to achieve a sense of safety and security by taking steps to protect themselves, such as changing their online profiles or blocking the bully's messages.

- **To restore and protect their reputation:** Cyberbullying can often damage a person's reputation, especially if false rumors or embarrassing photos or videos are shared online. Victims may hope to restore their reputations by clearing their names, issuing a public statement, or taking legal action if necessary.

- **To find support:** Victims of cyberbullying may hope to find support from friends, family, or professionals who can help them cope with the emotional impact of the bullying. They may also seek out online support groups or counseling services to get the help they need.

Overall, victims of cyberbullying hope to achieve a sense of safety, justice, and support and to put an end to the harassment they are experiencing.

GETTING TO KNOW THE ENEMY

Cyberbullies often hide behind anonymous or fake identities to protect themselves from being identified and held accountable for their actions. This anonymity emboldens them to engage in more aggressive and harmful behaviors online, such as spreading false information, making threats, and harassing their targets. It can also make it more difficult for their victims to defend themselves or seek help from authorities.

However, it is essential to note that anonymity does not always guarantee safety for cyberbullies. Law enforcement agencies and internet service providers can often trace their online activities and take legal action against them if their behavior is serious enough. In cases where cyberbullying behavior is directly threatening, it's essential to take immediate action to protect oneself and others. Suppose a cyberbully makes a direct threat or engages in harmful behavior. In that case, it's important to take screenshots of their posts or comments as evidence and report their behavior to the appropriate authorities.

Understanding the motivation behind cyberbullying is crucial in addressing the behavior. Cyberbullies may reveal their underlying motivations through their language, and skilled language use can help coax out their motivations. Based on my encounters with cyberbullies, here are the primary motivations I have identified:

- Seeking to enhance their online reputation by gaining "likes" and "followers."
- Reacting to actual or perceived offenses from others.
- Inflating their egos.
- Seeking to diminish the status of the victim or their group.
- Craving admiration.
- Trying to get even for a perceived wrong.
- Needing to feel important.
- Expressing anger.
- Exerting control.

IDENTIFYING AND AVOIDING CYBERBULLIES

This chapter will explore some tips for identifying and avoiding cyberbullies. I will discuss how to spot warning signs, protect your privacy, and stay safe online.

Firstly, not all cyberbullies are anonymous or hide behind fake identities. Sometimes, they can be people you know and call friends. Invariably, their motivation is one of those I mentioned previously.

These are some of the warning signs that you are a cyberbullying target.

1. Receiving threatening or abusive messages or comments online, including on social media platforms, email, or text messaging.
2. Experiencing frequent harassment or trolling on social media, such as being tagged in derogatory or humiliating posts or comments.
3. Seeing negative comments or rumors about yourself posted online can often spread quickly and be difficult to refute.

4. Feeling intimidated or forced into changing your point of view on a topic.
5. Constantly having your comments or posts unreasonably challenged, questioned, or denigrated in an attempt to belittle or humiliates you publicly.
6. Feeling anxious or depressed because of online harassment or bullying, including feeling like you can't escape the negativity even when you log off.
7. Experiencing changes in your behavior or mood, such as becoming more withdrawn or avoiding social situations.
8. Being excluded from online groups or communities or targeted by others in these groups.
9. Receiving unwanted sexual advances or messages online, which can be a form of cyberstalking or harassment.

As I mentioned, you cannot always 'run' or 'hide' from cyberbullying. However, this is some of the standard advice on how to protect your online security.

- **Use Strong Passwords:** Use strong passwords for all your online accounts and change them regularly. Avoid using the same password for multiple accounts.
- **Be Careful What You Share:** Be cautious about sharing personal information online, including your name, address, phone number, and email address. Avoid sharing personal information with people you do not know or trust.

- Limit Social Media Sharing: Be mindful of what you share on social media. Avoid sharing too much personal information, and be cautious about posting photos or videos that could be used against you.

- Set Privacy Settings: Use the privacy settings on your social media accounts to control who can see your posts and information.

- **Block and Report:** If you are being harassed or targeted by a cyberbully, block and report them on social media platforms. This will prevent them from being able to contact you or view your content.

- **Seek Help:** If a cyberbully is targeting you, seeking help from a trusted person or authority figure is essential. You can also reach out to support groups or hotlines for assistance.

Identifying and avoiding cyberbullies is crucial to protecting your online safety and well-being. Recognizing warning signs, protecting your privacy, and staying safe online can reduce your risk of being targeted by cyberbullies. Remember to seek help if you are being targeted, and do not hesitate to report harassment to the proper authorities.

TRACING A FAKE PROFILE

Tracing an anonymous fake Facebook profile can be difficult, but here are some steps you can take to try to identify the person behind the profile:

- **Collect information:** Gather as much information as possible about the fake profile. Take screenshots of any messages or posts, note details about the person's behavior or interactions, and gather other relevant information such as the profile picture, username, or location.
- **Report the profile:** Report the fake profile to Facebook. They have a team that investigates reports of fake profiles and may be able to take action to remove the profile or identify the person behind it.
- **Search for clues:** Find clues to help identify the person behind the fake profile. Check the profile's friends list, groups, and posts for any connections or information that could be useful. You can also try searching for the profile picture using Google's reverse image search to see if it appears on other websites.
- **Contact Facebook directly:** If you believe the fake profile is being used for illegal activities, such as harassment or identity theft, you can contact Facebook's legal department directly with your concerns.

PICKING A FAKE PROFILE

Here are some signs that may indicate that a Facebook profile is fake:

- **Profile picture:** The profile picture may be of a celebrity, model, or stock photo. The image may also look too good to be true or appear photoshopped.

- **Limited information:** The profile may need more information or more basic information. This may be because the person behind the profile is trying to hide their identity or because they created the profile quickly without providing much information.

- **Information:** Look at the information in the profile, such as the "about" section, education, and job history. Fake profiles may have incomplete or inconsistent information.

- **Recent account creation:** The account may have been created very recently, which may be suspicious if the person claims to be an old acquaintance or someone you know.

- **No or limited activity:** The profile may have little activity, such as only a few posts or interactions. This may be because the person behind the profile is not using it regularly or because they are using it to target specific people or groups.
- **Suspicious behavior:** The person behind the profile may behave suspiciously, asking for personal information or sending unsolicited messages. They may also be posting inappropriate or spammy content.
- **Friends list:** The person's friends list may be very small or consist of people you do not know or do not have any mutual friends with.

If you suspect that a Facebook profile is fake, you can try to gather more information about the person behind the profile, report the profile to Facebook, or simply ignore it and not engage with the person. It's always better to err on the side of caution and protect your personal information and online safety.

REASONS PEOPLE USE A FAKE PROFILE

There are several reasons why people hide behind fake profiles on social media. Here are some well-known reasons:

- **Anonymity**: People may want to remain anonymous on social media for various reasons, such as to avoid unwanted attention or harassment, to protect their privacy, or to express controversial opinions without fear of retaliation.

- **Impersonation**: Some individuals may use fake profiles to impersonate someone else, often with malicious intent, such as to defame or embarrass the person they are impersonating.

- **Scamming**: Fake profiles may also be used for fraud, such as to scam people out of money or personal information.

- **Trolling**: Trolls may use fake profiles to post inflammatory or off-topic messages to provoke others and cause disruption.

- **Catfishing**: Some people may create fake profiles to deceive others into forming romantic or emotional relationships with them.

- **Reputation management:** Individuals or companies may use fake profiles to manage their online reputation, such as to promote themselves or their products or to inflate their social media following artificially.
- **Propaganda**: Also called Astroturfing, which involves creating fake social media profiles, generating fake comments or reviews, or even creating entire websites or news outlets to spread a particular message or agenda. It is a form of deceptive marketing or propaganda that individuals, organizations, or even governments can use to manipulate public opinion or influence political outcomes.

IDENTIFYING AND AVOIDING CYBERBULLIES

This chapter will explore some tips for identifying and avoiding cyberbullies. I will discuss how to spot warning signs, protect your privacy, and stay safe online.

Firstly, not all cyberbullies are anonymous or hide behind fake identities. Sometimes, they can be people you know and call friends. Invariably, their motivation is one of those I mentioned previously.

These are some of the warning signs that you are a cyberbullying target.

1. Receiving threatening or abusive messages or comments online, including on social media platforms, email, or text messaging.
2. Experiencing frequent harassment or trolling on social media, such as being tagged in derogatory or humiliating posts or comments.
3. Seeing negative comments or rumors about yourself posted online can often spread quickly and be difficult to refute.

4. Feeling intimidated or forced into changing your point of view on a topic.

5. Constantly having your comments or posts unreasonably challenged, questioned, or denigrated in an attempt to belittle or humiliates you publicly.

6. Feeling anxious or depressed because of online harassment or bullying, including feeling like you can't escape the negativity even when you log off.

7. Experiencing changes in your behavior or mood, such as becoming more withdrawn or avoiding social situations.

8. Being excluded from online groups or communities or targeted by others in these groups.

9. Receiving unwanted sexual advances or messages online, which can be a form of cyberstalking or harassment.

As I mentioned, you cannot always 'run' or 'hide' from cyberbullying. However, this is some of the standard advice on how to protect your online security.

- **Use Strong Passwords:** Use strong passwords for all your online accounts and change them regularly. Avoid using the same password for multiple accounts.
- **Be Careful What You Share:** Be cautious about sharing personal information online, including your name, address, phone number, and email address. Avoid sharing personal information with people you do not know or trust.

- **Limit Social Media Sharing:** Be mindful of what you share on social media. Avoid sharing too much personal information, and be cautious about posting photos or videos that could be used against you.
- **Set Privacy Settings:** Use the privacy settings on your social media accounts to control who can see your posts and information.
- **Block and Report:** If you are being harassed or targeted by a cyberbully, block and report them on social media platforms. This will prevent them from being able to contact you or view your content.
- **Seek Help:** If a cyberbully is targeting you, seeking help from a trusted person or authority figure is essential. You can also reach out to support groups or hotlines for assistance.

Identifying and avoiding cyberbullies is crucial to protecting your online safety and well-being. Recognizing warning signs, protecting your privacy, and staying safe online can reduce your risk of being targeted by cyberbullies. Remember to seek help if you are being targeted, and do not hesitate to report harassment to the proper authorities.

STRATEGY

Depriving cyberbullies of their motivations can be an effective strategy for countering their attacks. However, attacking an anonymous person's self-belief can be challenging, as they may become defensive, dismissive, or even more offensive. Here are some legitimate methods you can use to reveal the flaws in their thinking:

- **Ask for evidence:** If someone claims to know more than you do, ask them to provide concrete evidence for their belief or allegation. Don't allow them to generalize; pick out one small piece of what they have written and stick to it until it has been fully explained. If they cannot provide any evidence, their opinion becomes irrelevant.

- **Use objective criteria:** Stick rigidly to the point and do not let them deflect or sway away from the facts. Use objective criteria to determine who has higher moral ground and standing in facts. For example, if someone claims to know more about a topic than you, ask that they show you how they got that knowledge. Following up with probing technical questions often exhausts the cyberbully.

- **Challenge assumptions:** If someone assumes they have a higher status than you based on factors such as inside knowledge, more information, or more experience, challenge those assumptions. Point out that these factors do not necessarily make their opinion or assumption correct.

- **Focus on mutual respect:** Instead of engaging in a power struggle over status, focus on mutual respect and collaboration. Emphasize that everyone has something valuable to offer and that no one person is inherently better than another.

Overall, these methods can help to address the motivations behind cyberbullying and reduce its impact on victims.

ESSENTIAL TOOLS

Figure 8 Persuasion method

The Figure 8 persuasion model is a communication technique developed by George Thompson, the founder of Verbal Judo, a program designed to help people effectively communicate under pressure. The Figure 8 persuasion model is based on the idea that effective communication involves a two-way exchange of ideas and emotions. The idea is that successful persuasion requires finding common ground with the other person.

The Figure 8 persuasion model consists of two loops or "circles," representing the communication exchange between two people. The first loop represents the message sent by the speaker, and the second loop represents the message received by the listener. The loops intersect in the middle, representing the point of common ground where the message is effectively communicated and understood.

The model involves eight key steps, which are as follows:

- **Loop one:** Empathize and gather information. The speaker should begin by showing empathy and attempting to understand the listener's perspective. The speaker should ask open-ended questions to gather information and encourage listeners to share their thoughts and feelings.

- **Intersection**: Find common ground. Once the speaker has gathered information and established a rapport with the listener, they should identify points of common ground between their perspectives. This intersection represents the point of agreement or understanding between the two parties.
- **Loop two:** Build the message. The speaker should use the information gathered from the listener to build a message tailored to their perspective. The message should be clear, concise, and focused on the common ground established in the intersection.
- **Intersection**: Deliver the message. The speaker should deliver the message in a way that is respectful and acknowledges the listener's perspective. The message should be designed to appeal to the listener's interests and values and should be delivered in a way that is clear and easy to understand.

By following the Figure 8 persuasion model, speakers can effectively communicate their message to the listener and persuade them to see things from their perspective. The model emphasizes the importance of empathy, active listening, and finding common ground, key components of effective communication.

Common ground refers to shared interests, values, or goals that people can agree on despite differing opinions or perspectives on certain issues. Finding common ground with someone who has yet to entirely agree with your opinion or viewpoint is possible.

For example, two people may have different opinions on addressing a perceived injustice. They may agree that the rule of law and equitable justice is important for society, but they may have other ideas about how justice was delivered in a particular case. They can work together to find answers that clarify specific points of law, which lead to a logical explanation of how a particular case was handled.

Finding common ground helps build respect for you and your point of view. It can open many lines of questioning that eventually lead to a logical conclusion. In the case of cyberbullying, it eventually exposes their emptiness and cowardice if they remain engaged with you for long enough.

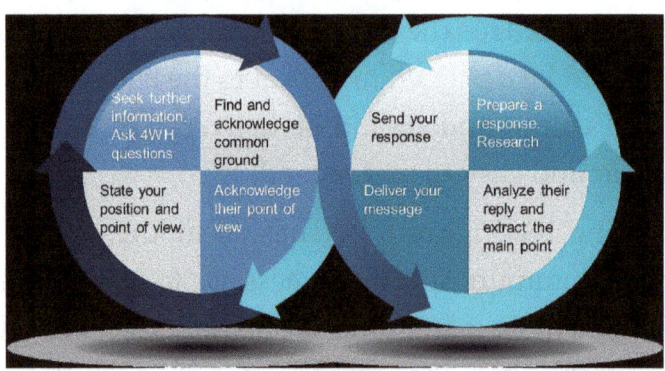

Figure 8 Persuasion Model

5WH Questions

Asking questions using the 5WH technique can be an effective strategy for disarming a cyberbully. By using these questions, you can gain a deeper understanding of the bully's motivations and thought process, which can help you to respond in a way that is more likely to de-escalate the situation.

Asking questions can also take the bully by surprise, as they often do not expect to be challenged this way. This can help disrupt their behavior pattern and create an opening for a more productive conversation.

Using the 5WH technique to ask questions can be a powerful tool for countering cyberbullying and promoting positive online interactions.

The five types of questions are:

- **Why**: Questions seeking to understand the topic's reasons or motivations. For example, "Why did you write that comment about me?"
- **What**: Questions seeking specific information about a particular aspect of the topic. For example, "What do you want me to do about that?"
- **Who**: Questions seeking to identify the people or groups involved in the topic. For example, "Who gave you that information?"
- **Where**: Questions seeking to identify the location or context of the topic. For example, "Where did you see me do that?"
- **When**: Questions seeking information about the time or frequency of an event or action. For example, "When did that take place?"

- **How**: Questions that seek information on how to do something or how something was done. For example, "How would you suggest I do that." "How did you get your information about me."

The 5WH question technique can be an effective tool for gaining a more specific understanding of a cyberbully's motivations. You can gain insights into the bully's thought process and intentions by asking questions about who, what, where, when, why, and how.

Additionally, the technique can help you identify potential inconsistencies in the bully's story, which may provide clues to their real identity if they use a fake one.

Using the 5WH technique to ask questions, you can gather more information and better understand the situation, which can help you respond more effectively.

ANGER AND AGGRESSION

Dealing with angry and aggressive individuals can be intimidating, but the experience can help you develop confidence and various techniques to handle multiple personality types and issues. As you gain more experience, you can become more skilled at navigating difficult situations and achieving positive outcomes.

Responding to cyberbullying can be incredibly challenging, but taking action to protect yourself and others from harm is essential. It is necessary because cyberbullying is a form of aggression that can escalate unchecked.

There is far too much information needed to fully explain the dynamics of human aggression in this book, so I will write about it as briefly as I believe is necessary to give you a basic understanding of how and why my cyberbully self-defense techniques work so well.

Anger: Aggression commonly originates from anger triggered by frustration, perceived threats, insults, attacks, or a need to correct a perceived wrong. Understanding these underlying emotions and triggers can help you craft targeted questions that uncover the real motives behind the attack.

By identifying the specific frustration, threat, insult, attack, or perceived wrong that triggered the attack, you can use the 5WH question technique and the Figure 8 persuasion strategy to address the root cause of the issue. This approach can help to resolve the problem at its source rather than engaging in endless arguments that only exacerbate the situation. Remember, addressing the underlying problem is key to effectively dealing with cyberbullying and is the beginning of the process of switching the focus back onto the bully.

Aggression: While it is true that aggression can be positive or negative, it is important to note that the concept of "positive aggression" is not commonly used or recognized in psychology or social sciences.

Instead, some researchers and scholars use the term "assertiveness" to refer to a behavior that is forceful but still respectful and focused on achieving a goal or constructively expressing one's needs. This behavior can be seen as positive, as it can help individuals to stand up for themselves and achieve their goals without resorting to harmful or abusive tactics.

On the other hand, "negative aggression" can refer to behaviors that are harmful, destructive, or intended to intimidate or control others. These behaviors are generally not respected or rewarded by society and can lead to negative consequences for both the aggressor and the victim.

This concept can be illustrated as follows.

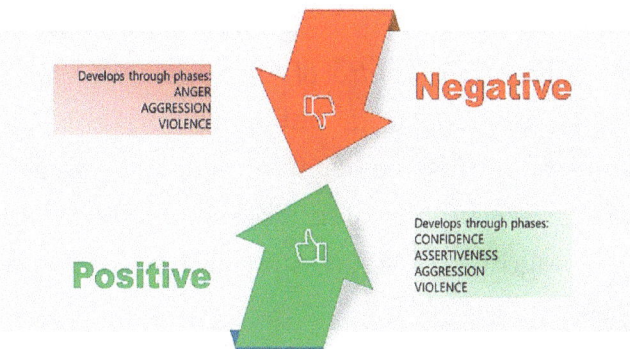

Development phases for positive and negative aggression

It's not uncommon for a cyberbully to try to turn the tables and accuse their victim of being the bully when they try to stand up for themselves. However, by understanding the dynamics of aggression, you can use this knowledge to your advantage and enhance your 5WH and Figure 8 strategies.

Don't let their accusations throw you off track - stay focused on your goal of protecting yourself and addressing the bullying behavior. Develop your positive aggression capabilities through knowledge, understanding, and practice.

Recognizing the subtle signs of aggression can be challenging, as many people only focus on demanding compliance. However, if you have a deeper understanding of the dynamics of human aggression and violence, you can identify risk factors and better predict the likelihood of aggressive behavior in an individual. This knowledge also helps you assess a person's aggression level and choose the most professional and effective approach to influence their behavior.

Arnold H Buss, *The Control of Aggression and Violence*, 1971 (Chapter 1) developed a table to present the three dichotomies of aggressive behavior: *physical – verbal*, *active – passive*, and *direct – indirect*. His table shows the interaction of the three categories of aggression and how they produce eight types.

	ACTIVE		PASSIVE	
	DIRECT	INDIRECT	DIRECT	INDIRECT
PHYSICAL	1.Assault	2.Damaging property	3. Obstructing, disruptive, or confronting behavior	4. Refusing to perform a necessary task
VERBAL	5.Insults, abuse, threats	6.Malicious gossip or rumor – verbal or written	7.Refusing to speak, rudeness, avoidance	8. Refusing consent – vocal or written, sullenness

Adapted from Arnold H. Buss, The Control of Aggression and Violence, 1971

The four active types of active aggression are easy to recognize, but the passive types are most often ignored in the traditional approaches to aggression management because they are less intense and therefore create less fear or concern.

If you can recognize each of these types of aggression in any given situation, it will assist you in identifying and choosing the appropriate style of response.

This table is a clear reminder that simply blocking, reporting, or avoiding a cyberbully may not be enough to end their attacks. As evidenced by the shift from direct to indirect attacks, it's clear that determined bullies will find ways to continue their harmful behavior regardless of attempts to hide from them. In short, it's important to take proactive steps to address the root of the issue rather than relying solely on avoidance measures.

AGGRESSIVE PERSONALITY TYPES

Understanding people's aggressive personality types can be helpful in working out how best to deal with them because it provides insights into their underlying motivations and behavior patterns. It can help you anticipate how they are likely to respond in different situations and provide you with strategies to defuse their aggression and maintain control of the situation.

For example, if you are dealing with a bulldozer type of person, you should focus on gathering facts and using their expertise to your advantage. Alternatively, avoid direct confrontation if you are dealing with a passive-aggressive person. Instead, focus on getting to the root of the issue and keeping the conversation issue-focused rather than personal.

By understanding how different aggressive personalities operate, you can develop more effective communication strategies that allow you to navigate challenging situations and manage difficult individuals more effectively.

Here are some of the common types I have encountered.

- **Charging** Bull describes hard-core personalities as hostile, abusive, and intimidating, always needing to be right and enjoy confrontation. They can be like angry bulls when challenged and enjoy intimidating others. The advice is to let them blow off steam and express their anger but draw the line if they become abusive. Maintaining control, addressing them by name, stating your position clearly, and avoiding losing self-control or arguing with them are important. Setting boundaries early on and speaking with calm assurance is key.

- **The Bulldozer** personality type is characterized by an overwhelming display of knowledge and facts, an arrogant and superior attitude, and a desire for attention and recognition. They can be difficult to deal with, but it is important to silence their overbearing chatter and engage in meaningful communication. To do this, it is necessary to know the facts and information, ask strategic questions to capitalize on their knowledge, and use praise to establish rapport. Continuing to probe their answers can eventually lead to silence, and from there, a more productive conversation can begin.

- **Sniper** types are passive-aggressive personalities who use sarcasm to undermine authority and criticize indirectly. They try to avoid open confrontations and may use the excuse of "just joking" to retract their comments if confronted. To deal with them, try to focus on the issues rather than personalities, and be direct in addressing the underlying problem. Once they realize that you won't tolerate their behavior, they will usually stop.

- **Defeatists** have a negative attitude and tend to complain and act defeated. They often feel unimportant, and their negativity is not based on logic. To deal with them, listen to what they say, steer them towards the facts, and focus on the positive aspects of the situation. Never debate their complaints or become involved in their emotions. Instead, maintain control and reinforce a positive outlook.

- **Whinger** describes people who constantly complain, distrust those in power, and only see the negative side of things. They believe their way is the only right way and often say, "I told you so." To deal with them, stay positive but realistic, avoid arguing, and stick to the facts. Reframe the conversation to focus on constructive solutions and emphasize the benefits of being a team player.

TURN THE OTHER CHEEK

"Turn the other cheek" is an idiom that comes from the Sermon on the Mount, where Jesus said, "Whoever slaps you on your right cheek, turn the other to him also." In societies with a Christian culture, even non-believers are familiar with this passage.

Most people believe the idiom means not retaliating against someone who has hurt you. People often say, "It's often best to turn the other cheek. Fighting won't solve the problem." I was raised with this idea but quickly learned it didn't work in the face of physical violence from schoolyard bullies.

As I faced online attacks, I followed the advice of experts, but it proved ineffective. Cyberbullies intensified their attacks. I realized that I had to fight back and thought of it as a self-defense problem. In physical self-defense, the level of force used must be both necessary and proportionate, and the burden of proof is on the person claiming self-defense to demonstrate that their actions were lawful and justifiable.

I researched ways to protect myself from cyberbullying but found no references to how victims could fight back for themselves. Protection seemed to need to come from someone else, and the advice to ignore or block the attacks was not effective and was interpreted as a sign of guilt or agreement by my attackers.

I delved deeper into the meaning of "turn the other cheek" and learned that it does not call for passiveness or acceptance of abuse or injustice. Instead, it calls for nonviolent resistance and moral courage. Turning the other cheek challenges the oppressor to recognize their wrongdoing and behave more justly and humanely.

The context in which the phrase was originally spoken is essential. In the time of Jesus, a slap on the right cheek was a social insult or a way of asserting power over another person. Turning the other cheek defied the oppressor's attempt to dominate and humiliate them.

Applying this principle to cyberbullying requires discernment and judgment. Fighting back does not necessarily mean engaging in a tit-for-tat or retaliatory way. Instead, it means taking a proactive and assertive stance in protecting oneself and asserting one's right to be treated with dignity and respect.

There have been times when my responses to some cyberbullies have been highly aggressive and threatening towards the cyberbully. In those cases, the principle of necessary and proportionate force was applied. I likened it to pulling back on the reins of a runaway horse until I had control over the conversation. However, I do not intend to dwell on that level of response in this book but may do so in the future in online training.

In summary, "Turn the other cheek" calls for nonviolent resistance and moral courage, not passivity or submission. Its meaning should be understood in its historical and cultural context, and its application requires careful discernment and judgment. Therefore, fighting against cyberbullying is necessary, justifiable, and the right thing to do. Not fighting back is morally corrupt.

HAVE COURAGE

Cyberbullying is a challenging situation that comes in many forms, and for some, it could be a difficult decision to engage with the attacker. Some people, particularly teenagers, can easily feel overwhelmed, scared, or unsure of what to do and what the bully might say or do next. However, it is important to remember that it is in these moments of uncertainty and fear that our courage is truly tested.

Having a clear vision of what is ahead, including the potential risks and rewards, can help empower us to act and face cyberbullies confidently. It is important to acknowledge that there may be dangers or difficulties ahead, but it is equally important to focus on the potential for benefits or success that may lie beyond those challenges.

When faced with a cyberbully attack, taking a step back and assessing the attack from a rational and objective perspective is essential. Consider the potential risks and rewards of taking action and weigh them against each other. Sometimes, the potential for benefit or success will outweigh the risks, and in those cases, it takes great courage to step forward and face the challenge.

Remember that courage is not about being fearless but rather about acknowledging your fears and pushing forward despite them. It is a willingness to take risks, to be vulnerable, and to confront uncertainty head-on. By embracing this mindset, we can develop the courage needed to face adversity and overcome it with strength and determination.

DIFFERENCE BETWEEN TECHNIQUES AND TACTICS

I should emphasize that am providing guidance on techniques in this book, not tactics.

Techniques and tactics are two different concepts that are often used interchangeably, but they have distinct meanings and applications.

Techniques refer to specific methods or procedures used to accomplish a particular task or goal. They are generally more concrete and tangible and can be learned through training or practice. For example, in martial arts, a technique might refer to a specific move, such as a punch or kick, that is used in combat.

Tactics, on the other hand, refer to broader strategies or plans used to achieve a larger objective. They are more abstract and strategic in nature and often involve considering a range of options and potential outcomes. For example, in a military context, a tactic might refer to a particular strategy for engaging with an enemy, such as a surprise attack or flanking maneuver.

In general, techniques are the specific actions or methods used to achieve a particular tactical objective. Tactics, on the other hand, are the broader plans or strategies that guide the use of those techniques to achieve a larger goal.

It is important to note that techniques and tactics are used in combination. In many situations, the choice of techniques used will depend on the tactical situation, and the overall strategy or plan will dictate which techniques are most appropriate. So, while they are distinct concepts, they are used together to achieve a desired outcome.

The tactics you use depend entirely on the situation you are faced with and your ability to employ them. If you liken a fight against a cyberbully to a game of chess, the verbal tactics you use are intended to force a move on your opponent to finally get to the point of checkmate. Checkmate is when the attack has been defeated, you have made your point, or the bully agrees with your point of view.

When considering tactics before going into a confrontation with an aggressive person, it's important to consider a range of factors that can affect the outcome of the situation. Here are some considerations to keep in mind:

- **Safety**: Your safety should be the top priority. Consider whether the situation is safe enough to engage in and whether any precautions need to be taken to ensure the safety of yourself and others who could be impacted.

- **Goals and objectives**: Determine your goals and objectives in the situation and what outcome you hope to achieve. This will help you to choose the most appropriate tactics and strategies to achieve your goals.
- **Knowledge of the other person**: Consider what you know about the other person's personality, behavior, and motives. This can help you to anticipate their actions and choose the most effective tactics to counter their behavior.
- **Power dynamics**: Consider the power dynamics of the situation, including any power imbalances or power differentials that may exist. This can help you choose appropriate tactics for the situation and avoid actions that may escalate the situation further.
- **Emotional intelligence**: It's important to be aware of your own emotions and reactions and those of the other person. Consider whether your own emotions may be influencing your behavior and whether you need to take steps to manage your emotions in the situation.
- **Communication skills:** Effective communication is key to diffusing tense situations. Consider what communication skills you can use to connect with the other person and create a more productive dialogue.
- **Flexibility**: Be prepared to adapt your tactics and strategies as the situation evolves. If one approach is not working, be open to trying a different approach.

By taking these considerations into account, you can approach the situation with a more strategic mindset and increase your chances of achieving a positive outcome.

If you need help and support for a specific situation, asking someone you know who is skilled in persuasive language and writing would be the best place to start.

SELF DEFENSE

Self-defense is not just about knowing how to fight back. It's about learning how to respond appropriately to different levels of aggression. Just like aggression can escalate or de-escalate, so can self-defense. It's essential to choose the right level of defense to match the level of aggression you're facing, whether it's a verbal attack or a physical assault. Responding excessively can worsen the situation, while responding with too little force may not be enough to stop the attacker.

By mastering the art of verbal self-defense, you can learn to suppress an attack with the appropriate level of forceful language, protecting yourself while avoiding unnecessary abuse and offense to the cyberbully or others.

These are some core principles of self-defense in general.

- **<u>Confidence</u>**: Confidence in yourself and your ability to defend yourself can help you stay calm and focused in a dangerous situation.
- **<u>Awareness</u>**: Being aware of your surroundings and potential threats can help you avoid dangerous situations before they occur.
- **<u>Avoidance:</u>** If possible, avoiding a potential threat is always the best course of action.

- **De-escalation:** If confronted with a potential threat, trying to de-escalate the situation through communication and non-violent means can effectively diffuse the threat.
- **Self-defense techniques:** Knowing and practicing self-defense can help protect yourself in a confrontation.
- **Use of force:** In a situation where physical force is necessary, using the appropriate level of force to defend yourself is essential. This includes understanding the laws and regulations surrounding self-defense in your area.

We can defend ourselves against cyberbullies by adapting these principles to verbal self-defense. With those principles in mind, let's consider appropriate types of response to a cyberbully attack.

RESPONDING TO AN ABUSIVE POST

Responding to an abusive online post can be challenging, and it's essential to approach the situation carefully to avoid making things worse. Here are some options for responding to an abusive online post:

- **Don't engage:** One of the best ways to respond to an abusive online post is not to respond. Engaging with the abuser can often escalate the situation, and it's important to remember that the person who posted the abusive comment is likely looking for a reaction. Sometimes the best response is no response.

- **Remain calm:** If you choose to respond, it's essential to remain calm and not let your emotions get the best of you. Reacting in anger or frustration can often worsen things and lead to further abuse. Take a deep breath, collect your thoughts, and respond calmly and rationally.

- **Be assertive:** When responding to an abusive online post, it's essential to be assertive and set clear boundaries. Let the person know that their behavior is unacceptable and that you will not tolerate it. Use "I" statements to express how their behavior affects you, such as "I feel hurt and disrespected by your comment."

- **Don't stoop to their level:** Responding to an abusive comment with insults or name-calling can be tempting, but this will only worsen the situation. Avoid stooping to the abuser's level and maintain your dignity and integrity in your response.

- **Report the abuse:** If it is severe or persistent, it may be necessary to report it to the platform or website where it occurred. Most platforms have a reporting feature that allows users to report abusive or inappropriate content. Documenting the abuse can help to protect yourself and others from further harm.

- **Ignore it:** Sometimes, the best way to deal with an abusive online post is to ignore it. This approach is beneficial when the post is not directed at you, and the content is not illegal or threatening. By ignoring the post, you can avoid further escalation and prevent the abuser from getting the attention they seek.

- **Block the abuser:** Most social media platforms allow users to block other users. If you're being harassed or bullied by someone, you can block them to prevent them from contacting you or seeing your posts. Blocking the abuser can help you to protect yourself from further harm.

- **Seek help:** Feeling overwhelmed and unsure how to respond is normal, especially if the attack is vicious or hurtful. Don't be afraid to ask for advice from someone you trust, whether a friend, a family member, or a professional. Take time crafting an appropriate, assertive response, but not aggressive or offensive. Remember, self-defense in the digital world is not about speed but about strategy and resilience.

RESPONDING ASSERTIVELY

If you choose to respond assertively to online abuse, here are some steps you can take:

- **Remain calm:** It's essential to remain calm and avoid getting defensive or angry. Responding with aggression or insults can escalate the situation and make it worse. Take some deep breaths and try to approach the situation with a clear mind.

- **Use "I" statements:** When responding to the abuser, use "I" statements to express how their behavior affects you. For example, "I feel hurt and disrespected by your comment" or "I find your language offensive and unacceptable." This approach can help to de-escalate the situation and avoid putting the abuser on the defensive.

- **Set boundaries:** Let the abuser know that their behavior is unacceptable and that you will not tolerate it. Be clear about your boundaries and what behavior you expect from them. For example, "I will not tolerate name-calling or insults, and I will not engage in this conversation unless you can be respectful."

- **Stick to the facts:** Avoid making assumptions or accusations and stick to the facts. If the abuse is related to a specific issue, present the facts and your perspective. Avoid making personal attacks or getting sidetracked by irrelevant details.

- **End the conversation if necessary:** If the abuser continues to be abusive or refuses to respect your boundaries, it may be best to end the conversation. Let them know you have made your point. A good time to end the conversation is when you feel that you have made your point and there is no further productive dialogue. If the conversation is becoming repetitive or is going in circles,

BOUNDARIES TO SET AND ABIDE BY

When dealing with online abuse, here are some boundaries you can consider setting:

- **No name-calling or insults:** It's crucial to keep your cool and avoid retaliating with insults or name-calling, as this only fuels the cycle of aggression and makes you look as bad as the bully. Responding calmly and assertively while focusing on the content of the attack will allow you to address the problem without resorting to bad language. By responding respectfully, you demonstrate your strength and make it clear that you won't tolerate any form of abusive conduct.

- **No threats or intimidation:** Be assertive without resorting to threats or intimidation. Being assertive means standing up for yourself and expressing your feelings and boundaries clearly and confidently while respecting the other person's right to courtesy. It's important to avoid using overly harsh, aggressive language or making personal attacks, as this can escalate the situation and make it more challenging to resolve. Instead, focus on addressing the content in the conversation causing the problem and making it clear that it is wrong and unacceptable.

- **No hate speech or discrimination:** Responding to a cyberbully with hate speech or discriminatory language only lowers us to their level and diminishes the credibility of our response. It is essential to maintain our values and beliefs by responding in a respectful and non-discriminatory manner. By doing so, we demonstrate that we will not stoop to their level and that we are above such behavior. In addition, responding with respect and kindness may help de-escalate the situation and encourage the cyberbully to reconsider their behavior.

Setting clear boundaries and showing good behavior are essential when responding to cyberbullying. However, it is also important to show that you are listening to the other person's perspective, even if they are wrong. This indicates that you are willing to engage in a dialogue and find a solution.

SAMPLE QUESTIONS

When dealing with a bully who is making negative comments or accusations about you, it can be tempting to react emotionally or defensively. However, it's important to remember that the bully's goal is likely to provoke a reaction from you and engaging with them on their terms can give them power over the situation.

One way to shift the dynamic is to ask questions that force the bully to explain their thinking and actions. This can be done non-confrontational, showing you are interested in understanding their perspective rather than being defensive.

By asking questions, you also burden the bully with proof to justify their accusations or comments. This can be a powerful tool in demonstrating that you know the truth and have a high moral ground. It also forces the bully to engage in a conversation that they may not be prepared for, which can throw them off balance and give you an opportunity to regain control of the situation.

Some examples of questions you could ask include:

- What makes you think that?
- Can you explain your reasoning?
- How did you come to that conclusion?

- Can you provide evidence to support your claim?
- What specific actions or behaviors of mine are you referring to?
- How do you think your comments are affecting me?
- Have you considered how others might interpret your words?
- Can you tell me more about why you feel this way?
- What do you hope to achieve by saying these things to me?
- How would you feel if someone said those things to you?

Remember to stay calm and respectful in your tone, even if you feel frustrated or upset. The goal is to shift the dynamic and assert your own sense of control over the situation rather than engaging in a back-and-forth argument with the bully.

CONCLUSION

Cyberbullying is a harmful and cowardly act that has the potential to cause significant harm to its victims. It takes many different forms, including sending threatening or harassing messages, spreading rumors or lies, creating fake profiles or accounts, sharing embarrassing or private information, and more. These acts are often carried out anonymously, making it difficult to identify the perpetrators and hold them accountable for their actions.

The motives behind cyberbullying can vary from jealousy and envy to revenge and anger. Sometimes it is done for entertainment purposes or to gain social status among peers. Regardless of the motive, cyberbullying is never justified and should be treated as a serious offense.

Victims of cyberbullying often feel powerless, vulnerable, and isolated. They may experience a range of negative emotions, including anxiety, depression, and low self-esteem. The effects of cyberbullying can be long-lasting and may even lead to physical harm or self-harm.

To prevent cyberbullying from occurring, it is crucial to establish a zero-tolerance attitude for this behavior. This means that individuals who engage in cyberbullying should be held accountable for their actions, and appropriate consequences should be imposed. It also involves creating safe and supportive environments in which victims of cyberbullying can seek help and support without fear of further harm.

In conclusion, cyberbullying is a harmful and cowardly act that should not be tolerated in any form. By understanding its nature, motives, and effects, we can take steps to prevent cyberbullying from occurring and protect its victims from harm. We must all work together to create a safe and supportive environment where everyone can thrive without fear of harassment or abuse.

The Cyberbully Self-Defense Handbook provides a valuable resource for anyone who has experienced cyberbullying or wants to protect themselves from its harmful effects. By understanding the nature of cyberbullying and the tactics used by cyberbullies, readers can learn how to confront this type of aggression assertively and effectively. The guide emphasizes the importance of seeking support from trusted sources and building resilience in the face of adversity. With the right mindset and tools, anyone can defend themselves against cyberbullying and emerge stronger and more empowered.

EXAMPLES OF CYBERBULLYING

1996-2016
20 YEARS CORRUPTION, DECEPTION, LIES
OFFICIAL MASS MURDER, PORT ARTHUR, TASMANIA

MICHAEL (*Mick/Rick*) DYSON
Tasmania Police

A "Now look at the time that Michael Charles Dyson, be he a sergeant or an acting inspector adopted this statement. This statement was adopted by Dyson on 12 September 1996, 4½ months [139 days] after the incident. Now this is not only extremely sloppy, but it is the first sign that this statement is a fabrication. In any normal court procedure, **this statement by Dyson would be thrown out as completely unreliable.**" (added emphasis)

B "The differences in each of these three *searches* is remarkable and defies logic in every way except for the conclusion that most of the *evidence* found at 30 Clare Street* had to have been planted there by police, and **we have Dyson's admission that it was he who planted much of that evidence**. It is thus worthwhile for the reader to compare the statements of sergeant Michael Charles Dyson with the relevant portion of the *Statutory Declaration* made by sergeant Gerard Dutton. The anomalies will astound you." (added emphasis) * Martin Bryant's home in Hobart which was, like all his financial assets, stolen from him by the State.

C "One of those employees of the State whom we are to believe is a meticulous teller of truths is **Michael Charles Dyson**. We are to believe he knows nothing about the Port Arthur incident beyond what he learnt as a 'liaison officer' during the incident. Sounds good, but.... *Mick* has a reputation.... It seems Dyson likes violence.... This is how Dyson describes his real interest: 'I was being given an opportunity to go to the more strategic level and become involved in the overall command of **violent incidents** which is my passion.' So we have a man who not only likes being involved with violent incidents, but one who tells the world he has a passion to be involved with death and destruction." (added emphasis)

D "In regard to the Port Arthur Massacre, the most violent incident ever to occur within Australia, let alone Tasmania, the first and only time that the Plans for an 'Anti-Terrorist' situation were implemented, Sergeant Michael Dyson, the former SOG Assault Team Leader, the only SOG member with any siege experience, was not available to assist the SOGs in their part of the exercise, and the required drills that had been planned by Dyson.... We are aware that Martin Bryant had a mate with him in Seascape Cottage, a mate called *Rick*.... We are also aware that whoever was with Martin, that person was well aware of the various tactics and drills performed by the Tasmania Police SOGs, and had similar equipment to the SOGs such as night viewing equipment, and laser sights. This equipment was not discovered in the charred ruins of Seascape Cottage, and so presumably must have left with *Rick*." ∎

MICHAEL DYSON
"...command of violent incidents which is my passion"

- 17 -

Example of a propaganda publication using a stolen image

OFFICIAL KILLING IN TASMANIA, AUSTRALIA

Forthcoming book on innocent Martin Bryant who was denied a trial and who is now imprisoned until he dies for crimes he did not commit in Tasmania, Australia.

TUESDAY 2 APRIL 2013   EMAIL, LINK, WEBSITE

– MICHAEL DYSON –
aka *Mick/Rick, Jamie, Gunman of Seascape*; ex *Son of God*
mdyson@calypto.com.au; Hobart, Tasmania, Australia

An email bearing the name Michael Dyson and requesting book-related information has been received. This writer has no way of knowing if it is genuine. Regardless, recipients of this correspondence are informed the book *MASS MURDER: Official Killing in Tasmania, Australia* will be released by the middle of this year. The release was planned for 7 May – Martin Bryant's birthday. But the increase in case-related documents and information* being sent to me has slowed the completion process.

Dyson was, it seems, a key player in the official killing at Port Arthur in April 1996: **35 people murdered and 23 wounded**. The book contains details about him, his Internet WANTED poster, and his revealing words: "I was being given an opportunity to...become involved in the overall command of violent incidents which is my passion...." It seems Dyson **planned the massacre and was at Seascape when Glenn Pears & David and Sally Martin were killed there on Sunday 28 April 1996.** An official in Hobart has provided me with notes showing Mrs. Martin was not killed by Bryant as asserted by the mongrel DPP, Damian Bugg.

Finally, if the email is from Dyson it seems he plans to intimidate me, as Tasmania Police and Avery** tried (in vain) to intimidate Terry Hill. All publicity is positive. Related details will be included in the book.***
It seems the official killing is troubling this Michael Dyson and his daughter. It will be a loss if he tops himself – we need him alive, not dead.

Sincerely,

*   **A QUESTION OF GUILT: Could he really be guilty?** (video):
Sunrise A.V. Productions, Box 642, Nanango, QLD 4615   nannews@burcom.com.au

**   **The Mercury** (28 SEP 2012) published this about that CRIMINAL lawyer: "[John Avery] pleaded guilty in 2008 to 130 counts of stealing and dishonesty between December 2001 and March 2006. He admitted stealing more than $500,000 from his clients and his former law firm at Moonah (Hobart) to support his obsession with art and luxury. His victims included those who had won personal injury or workers' compensation claims and a survivor of the 1964 HMAS Voyager disaster."

see: indymedia.org.au/2012/10/01/martin-bryant-is-innocent (over 6000 hits)

***   candobetter.net/files/DRAFT.PART5_.MASS_.MURDER.TAS_.AUS_.pdf

Dr. Keith Allan Noble
author: *FIND! FALCONIO – Dead or Alive*
free pdf copy: manuals4u.com.au/about-us/25k-reward/
Unit 72 B, Am Heumarkt 7, 1030 Vienna, Austria t/f: 43-1-9712401
MURDER.RESEARCH@gmail.com, BIGWORMBOOKS@gmx.net

EUREKA STOCKADE *– series –*

The author was accused of being intimidating after challenging the publication.

Fabricated newspaper front page circulated in Facebook posts.

Trolling profile

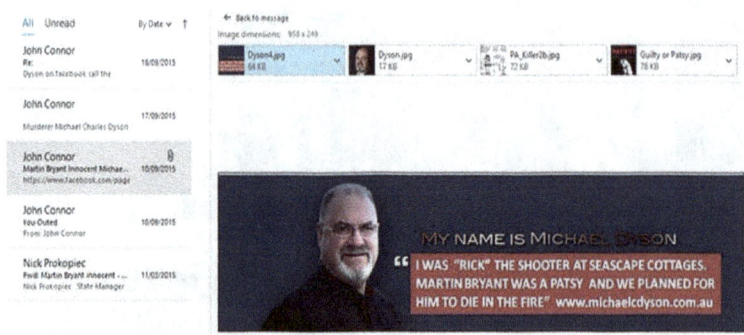

Stolen image used to create a Facebook page

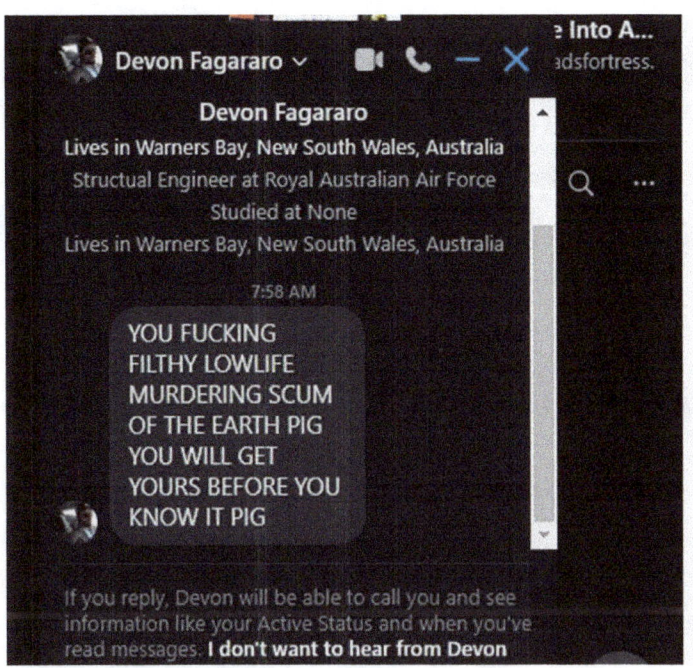

 Solar Man
You and Solar aren't connected on Facebook
Lives in Bangkok, Thailand

APR 14, 2019, 9:54 PM

 How is the port Arthur killer these days.

APR 18, 2019, 6:49 PM

 You look like an evil prick

MAY 15, 2019, 10:35 AM

 Coming to get you fuck

Abusive SMS messages

EXAMPLES INCLUDING RESPONSES

> Will you put your comment back up with a full apology?

well im pretty sure you said you'd sue me not that i got anything as the ex.wife cleaned me out good and proper

it has been pulled down

it will not be put back up on any medium i surf

You can now call each other and see information like Active Status and when you've read messages.

> All other people who make that allegation had no money or hid behind false identities. You are lucky.
>
> However, I am almost finished writing a book about this and how to deal with cyber bullying. I intend to use this screen shot in the book to show how that it never stops. Is that ok with you.

no, my permission is not granted michael for your book however i will promise to buy it if you choose to let me know the name of it now or when completed - i may change my view on pt.auther

conspiracy Theories exists because we the people know we've been fed crap on all sorts of issues from pt.aurther to 9/11 to the Illuminati and Freemasonry and corrupted governments world wide we all suffer under

have you see yourself on YouTube ?

> I will redact your name, but use the comment and picture.
> I have been dealing with this since email began and before. I have read all the stuff, spoke to or corresponded with many authors, been interviewed by a movie producer and more. All are no longer believe I was the shooter. Martin Bryant's mother was with me while he was holed up in Seascape. I searched his house with her.
> The stuff you read about me is very, very old and is regurgitated as new people come along that are sucked in by the theory.

critical thinking capacity's along with i.q levels
because you never know who knows what

im happy for you to retract my name in your book

- let me know what's it's called, ill buy it, study it's contents and
you may never know - you may change my view

take care of yourself michael

> Thanks. But I can't support your views on conspiracy theories

* * * *

www.ingramcontent.com/pod-product-compliance
Lightning Source LLC
Chambersburg PA
CBHW071228160426
43196CB00012B/2456